ART AARDVARK

WRITTEN BY ROBERTA WEST-NAUS
ILLUSTRATED BY BEV ARMSTRONG

The
Learning
Works

Edited by Sherri M. Butterfield

The purchase of this book entitles the individual teacher to reproduce copies for use in the classroom.

The reproduction of any part for an entire school or school system or for commercial use is strictly prohibited.

No form of this work may be reproduced or transmitted or recorded without written permission from the publisher.

To the Teacher

The Art Aardvark is designed to create an awareness of basic art techniques and a familiarity with basic art materials for students in grades K-8. The activities have been selected to stimulate interest, foster creativity, encourage self-expression, and develop an appreciation for a variety of methods and media. Because the instructions have been written with students in mind, these activities will require very little preparation time.

The grade level listed for each individual lesson in the table of contents is intended as a general guide only. You are the best judge of what activities are appropriate for the members of your class. For younger children, you may wish to precut the materials and to supply patterns or finished examples.

The Art Aardvark is divided into five main sections, entitled Paper, Gift Ideas, Fabrics and Textures, Paints, and Prints. The contents and emphases of these sections are summarized below.

1. **Paper.** Students are led to explore and use this versatile medium by bending, cutting, curling, folding, gluing, pressing, and rubbing.

2. **Gift Ideas.** Students are given complete instructions for a variety of special-occasion gifts, including soap balls, banners, decorative bottles, collages, greeting cards, and stitchery samplers.

3. **Fabrics and Textures.** Students employ a variety of surfaces and media to create and explore texture. Complete instructions are given for twenty different projects (with suggested variations), including rubbings of several types, string dolls, crayon, batik, and yarn painting.

4. **Paints.** Students use inks, oil base pastels, tempera paints, and watercolors, which they apply with everything from conventional brushes to unconventional empty roll-on deodorant containers and Q-tips.

5. **Prints.** Students learn how to use brayer rollers and how to construct printing blocks. They also have an opportunity to print directly from a variety of textured objects, such as fruits, leaves, sandpaper, and vegetables.

Illustrated, step-by-step directions are given for each project in this book. In all instances, they describe the process thoroughly but leave the results entirely to the creative imagination of the student.

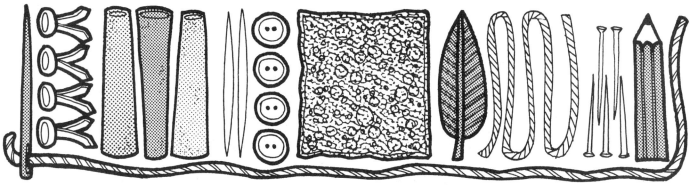

Contents

Fabrics and Textures

Paints

Prints

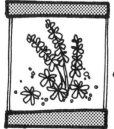  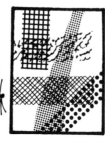  

Name _____

Design Your Own Puzzle

What You Need

12″ x 18″ piece of white construction paper
pencil
scissors
white glue
12″ x 18″ piece of tagboard
black, broad-tipped marking pen

What You Do

1. With a pencil, draw lines to divide your paper into irregularly shaped "puzzle pieces" as shown.

2. Using scissors, cut the paper on the pencil lines.

3. Write your name on each puzzle piece.

4. Turn all of the pieces over and color each one separately. You may wish to limit your choice of colors to only three and repeat these same colors in the design you create on each piece. Work different shapes or figures into each piece and color with dark, heavy strokes.

5. After all of the pieces have been colored, put your puzzle together again and watch the design you have created emerge.

6. Glue the finished puzzle pieces, name side down, to a piece of tagboard.

7. Add contrast by outlining each piece with a black, broad-tipped marking pen.

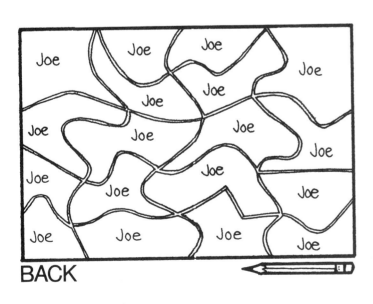

BACK

FRONT

Name _____

3-D Paper Strip Flowers

What You Need

pieces of construction paper in colors suitable for flower petals, centers, leaves, and stems
scissors
white glue
9″ x 12″ pieces of construction paper for background

What You Do

1. Cut several ½-inch by 6-inch strips from construction paper.

2. Fold each strip and glue the insides of the ends together to make a loop. (If you glue inside to outside, you'll get a circle.)

3. Glue these loops onto your piece of construction paper in a circle as shown so that they resemble the petals of a daisy or other similar flower.

4. Add stems (strips) and leaves (loops of a different color and, perhaps, a slightly different length or width).

5. Cut a circle from a contrasting color of construction paper.

6. Glue it over the glued ends of the petals to form the center of the flower.

Just for Fun

Experiment with different sizes of loops and different styles of petals, centers, and stems.

Pinwheels

What You Need

    lightweight paper (ditto paper works well)
    pencil
    scissors
    straight pin
    pencil with eraser *or* plastic straw
    crayons *or* felt-tipped marking pens

What You Do

1. Draw a 6-inch by 6-inch square on the lightweight paper.

2. Cut it out.

3. Draw diagonal lines from each corner to the opposite corner.

4. Draw a circle (about one inch in diameter) at the center where the diagonal lines cross.

5. Mark four corners as shown with the numbers 1, 2, 3, and 4.

6. Cut the diagonal lines up to the center circle.

7. One at a time, bend—but do not fold— each numbered corner toward the center.

8. Overlap these corners, and push a pin through them and then through the center of the circle.

9. Push the pin into a drinking straw or the eraser of your pencil.

10. Adjust the pinwheel until it spins.

11. Using felt-tipped marking pens or crayons, draw designs on your pinwheel. Flatten out the paper first, and then create your design. Experiment with the three primary colors—red, yellow, and blue. What happens to your design and the colors when the pinwheel spins?

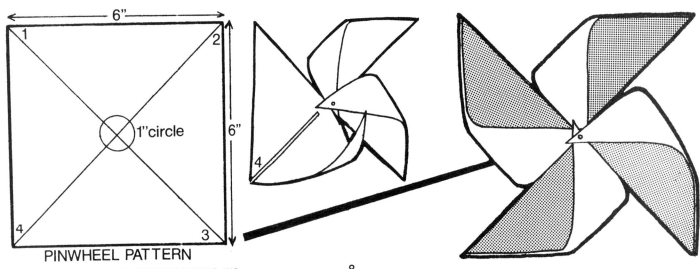

PINWHEEL PATTERN

Name _____

3-D Paper Shapes

What You Need

any moderately stiff paper, white or colored (avoid papers as thin as tissue and newsprint)
scissors
glue
crayons or felt-tipped marking pens

What You Do

1. From the paper, cut a basic shape as shown.

2. Bend the ends around to form a circle. Look carefully at the bent shape. What does it resemble? What animal or figure does it suggest?

3. Flatten the shape and draw features on it to show what it suggests to you.

4. Bend the shape once again, and glue the ends in place.

5. Try different patterns and shapes. Construct a zoo of animals, a collection of funny people, a neighborhood of unusual houses.

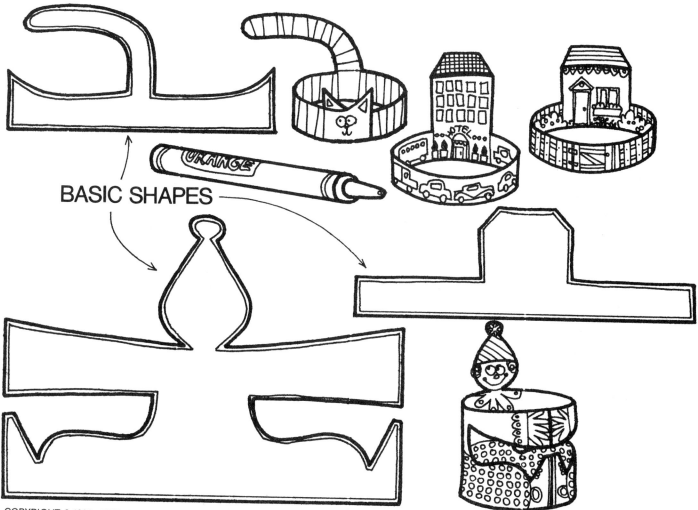

BASIC SHAPES

9

Name _____

Accordion-Pleated Animals

What You Need

  construction paper
  scissors
  white glue
  felt-tipped marking pens

What You Do

1. Cut construction paper into 2-inch by 12-inch strips.

2. Accordion fold each strip.

3. From construction paper scraps, cut a head and tail for an animal. (See patterns on page 11.)

4. Glue the head to one end of your pleated paper and the tail to the other end.

5. Using felt-tipped marking pens or paper cutouts, add eyes, nose, and other appropriate features.

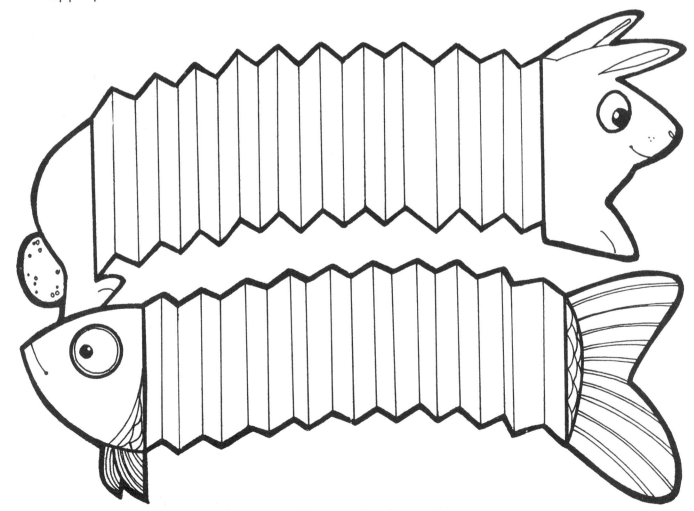

Head and Tail Patterns
for
Accordion-Pleated Animals

11

Name _____

Negative/Positive Space: Lines That Move

What You Need

> construction paper
> scissors
> white glue
> hole punch
> string or yarn

What You Do

1. Select two colors of construction paper. Use color opposites for a more dramatic effect.

2. Cut construction paper into two 6-inch by 6-inch squares or two 6-inch by 8-inch rectangles.

3. On one piece of construction paper, draw a wavy, jagged, or zigzagging line from one corner to the opposite corner.

4. Cut along this line so that you will have two separate pieces.

5. Glue one cut piece to one side of the uncut piece of construction paper.

6. Turn the construction paper over and glue the second cut piece to the other side.

7. Punch a hole in the top. Put a piece of string or yarn through the hole and tie it.

8. Hang your design from the ceiling or from a line strung across the room.

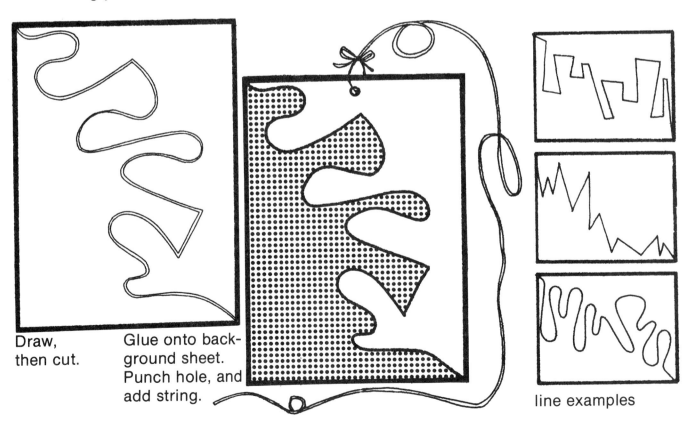

Draw, then cut.

Glue onto background sheet. Punch hole, and add string.

line examples

Name _____

Chalk and Shapes

What You Need

pencil
4" x 4" tagboard squares
colored chalk
scissors
white paper in different sizes but larger than 4" x 4"
colored paper for mounting

What You Do

1. Using a pencil, draw simple designs on three or four pieces of tagboard.

2. With the scissors, cut out the shapes you have drawn.

3. Rub chalk along the edges of your tagboard shapes.

4. Place each shape on white paper, hold it down firmly with one hand, and use the fingers of your other hand to brush chalk from the shape onto the white paper. Do this around the entire shape.

5. Remove the shape.

6. Rub chalk on the shape again and repeat step 4 as many times as are necessary to create a design you like.

Variations

Experiment with different colors of chalk and different combinations of shapes. Try overlapping shapes to create designs.

Suggested Uses

Use the designs you create with chalk and shapes as pictures, to decorate cards or wrapping paper, or as backgounds for other artwork.

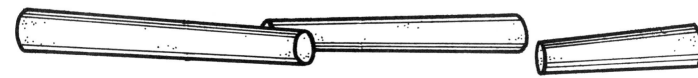

13

Name _____

Wet Chalk Designs

What You Need

newsprint
sponge
large-sized chalk in assorted colors (Bright colors highlighted with black work nicely.)
plastic container (margarine tub, bowl, etc.)
clear shellac
paintbrush
white glue
construction paper sheets for backing

What You Do

1. Lay newsprint on a table. With a wet sponge, completely saturate the paper with water.

2. Put chalk in plastic container. Partly fill the container with water. Keeping the chalk moist while you work will prevent you from getting chalk dust smudges on your paper.

3. Using the flat of the chalk and making broad, sweeping strokes, create a picture or pattern on the newsprint.

4. Allow the paper to dry completely.

5. Lightly brush shellac over the design and allow to dry. The shellac will give your design an oil paint look.

6. Glue the design to colored construction paper.

Name _____

Stained Glass

What You Need

black paper
pencil
scissors
colored tissue paper
white glue

What You Do

1. Fold black paper in half.

2. With a pencil, draw the outside shape of an object on one side of the black paper.

3. Cut out the folded shape using pencil line as a guide.

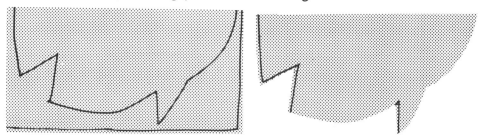

4. Now draw holes inside the shape, leaving space around the holes.

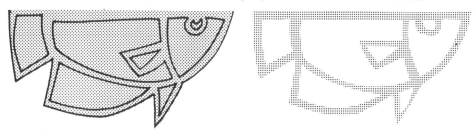

5. Using scissors, cut out the holes you have drawn, being careful to cut through both thicknesses of paper and *not* to cut through the folded edge.

6. Cut pieces of tissue paper a little larger than the holes.

7. Glue the tissue paper over the holes in *one* side of your black paper.

8. Fold the black paper back the way it was and glue the open edges together.

Suggested Uses

Depending on their size and theme, you can use your stained glass designs as tree ornaments, parts of mobiles, or window trim.

15

Name _____

Torn Tissue Paper Pictures

What You Need

liquid starch
wide-mouthed plastic container *or* paper cup
tissue paper of various colors
broad-tipped paintbrush
one 9″ x 12″ piece of white construction paper
one larger piece of colored construction paper

What You Do

1. Pour starch into a cup or other suitable wide-mouthed container.

2. Tear tissue paper of various colors into irregular shapes.

3. Dip the brush in the starch. Then apply starch to the white construction paper where you want to put the first piece of tissue paper.

4. Select a piece of tissue paper and lay it smoothly on the wet starch.

5. Brush the top of the tissue paper piece with starch.

6. Repeat steps 3, 4, and 5 until your picture is complete. For an interesting effect, overlap tissue paper of various colors.

7. Allow your picture to dry.

8. Mount your finished picture on a larger piece of colored construction paper so that the colored paper provides both a backing and a frame.

Suggested Uses

A picture created by assembling bits and pieces from a single medium (for example, paper) is called a **montage.** Use this technique to create decorative pictures and cards, placemats and murals.

Name _____

"Exploded" Geometric Shapes

What You Need

pencil
two 9" x 12" pieces of construction paper in contrasting colors
one larger piece of construction paper in a complementary color
scissors
white glue

What You Do

1. Select a single sheet of colored construction paper.

2. With a pencil, draw two or three basic shapes on the paper.

3. Working with one shape at a time, cut the shapes apart as shown.

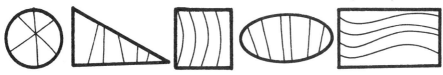

4. Glue shapes in original form (but separated, or "exploded") onto a second sheet of construction paper of a contrasting color.

5. Mount the finished picture on a third sheet of construction paper. This sheet should be larger than 9 inches by 12 inches so that it will provide both a backing and a frame for your exploded-shape picture. For a pleasing appearance, select paper of a complementary rather than contrasting color for the frame.

Name _____

Paper Curls

What You Need

    construction paper in a variety of colors
    scissors
    pencil
    white glue

What You Do

1. Cut strips ¼ inch wide and 8 inches long from construction paper of various colors.

2. Wrap each strip tightly around a pencil.

3. Slide the curled paper off the pencil.

4. Dip one edge of the curled paper into a small amount of white glue.

5. Place the curl on another sheet of construction paper.

6. Repeat steps 2, 3, 4, and 5 to form a design of curls. See illustrations for design ideas.

Variation

    Cut a shape from construction paper, glue it onto the backing sheet, and then *fill in* this shape with paper curls in a matching or contrasting color.

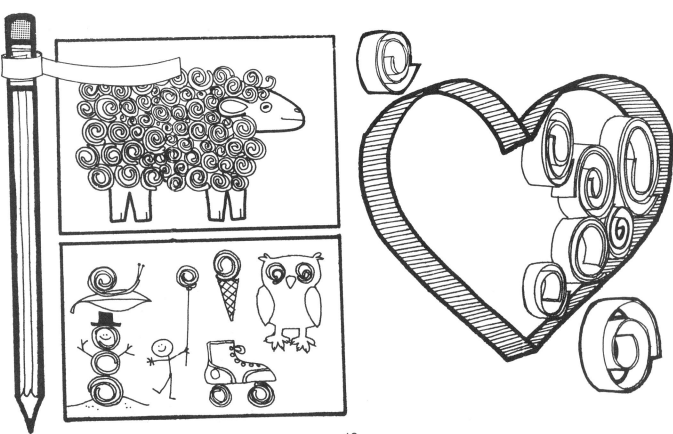

Name _____

Folded/Cut Paper Design (Paper Relief)

What You Need

two 9″ x 12″ pieces of construction paper in different colors
scissors
white glue

What You Do

1. Fold one sheet of paper into four sections as shown.

2. Cut the paper on one folded side. Then cut along the opposite folded edge in a continuing pattern. Do not remove cut sections.

3. Unfold the cut paper.

4. Glue the cut sheet onto a second sheet of a different color. Glue along the edges only—otherwise the flaps won't open.

5. Fold the cut sections down so that the second sheet shows through the first.

Suggested Uses

Using this method, create wall decorations and greeting cards.

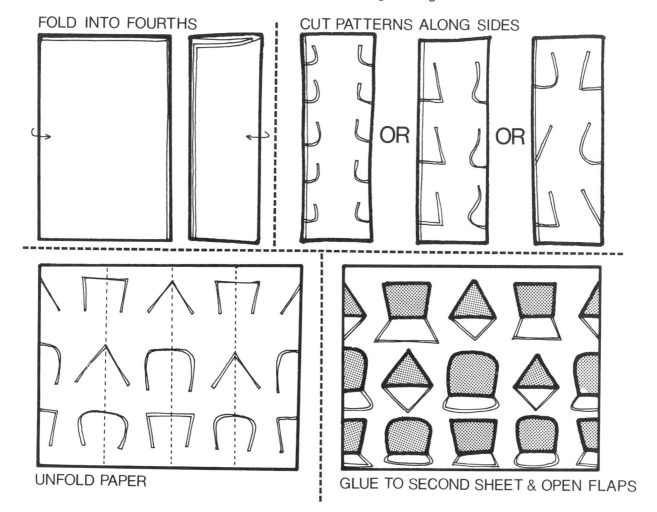

FOLD INTO FOURTHS

CUT PATTERNS ALONG SIDES

OR   OR

UNFOLD PAPER

GLUE TO SECOND SHEET & OPEN FLAPS

Name _____

Triangle Figure

What You Need

pattern on page 21
scissors
one 7½″ x 7½″ piece of construction paper
pencil
white glue

What You Do

1. Using the pattern on page 21, draw two large triangles (not equilateral), one small triangle, and one circle on a piece of construction paper.

2. Glue the parts in place to form a figure as shown.

3. From the remaining scraps, cut and add feathers to the hat, features to the face, feet, hands, and/or buttons on the shirt.

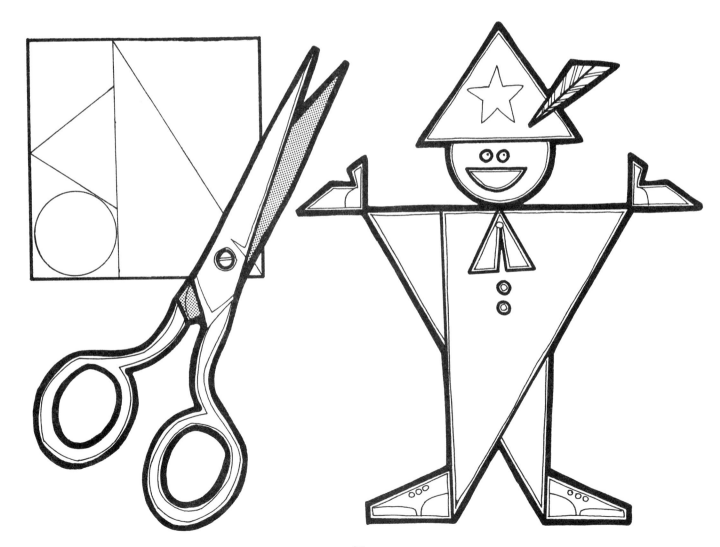

Triangle Figure Pattern

circle for head

cut

cut

triangle
for
hat

cut

cut

scrap for
hands,
feet,
feather,
buttons for shirt

Passing-Time Pictures

What You Need

one 6″ x 18″ strip of white paper
crayons, pencils, pens, or paint for drawing and coloring

What You Do

1. Fold your strip so that you get four equal spaces.

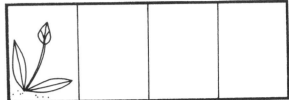

2. Draw the beginning part of a design or picture in the first space.

3. In each of the next three spaces, add to your picture until you finish it in the last space.

4. Mount or frame your strip.

Variations

1. Show how a flower bud forms, begins to unfold, and then opens up completely.

2. Illustrate how a person walks, a baby crawls, or a colt stands.

3. Fold your strip so that you get five equal spaces. Then draw the sun at sunrise, at 10:00 a.m., at noon, at 4:00 p.m., and at sunset.

Name _____

Paper Weaving

What You Need

one sheet of colored construction paper
additional construction paper to cut in strips
scissors
white glue

What You Do

1. For background, fold paper in half. Draw a line one inch from the edge opposite the folded side.

2. Draw straight or wavy lines from folded edge to one-inch line. Cut along these lines.

3. From construction paper the same size as the first but using a different color, cut strips about one inch wide. Cut these strips in the direction perpendicular to the way you draw and cut the lines on the background paper. For example, if you cut the background horizontally, cut the strips vertically.

4. Unfold the background sheet.

5. Choose a strip to weave through.

6. Starting on one side, slide this strip alternately under one background strip and over the next.

7. When you have woven a strip from one side to the other, push it toward the edge and make the ends even.

8. Do the same with second strip but this time go over and then under.

9. Repeat steps 5, 6, 7, and 8 until the background space is full.

10. Trim the ends of the strips if necessary and glue them down.

Suggested Uses

Weave paper to make baskets, place mats, lampshades, and wall hangings.

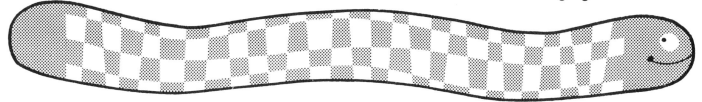

Name _____

Paper Birds

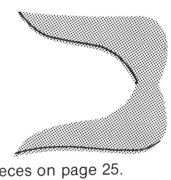
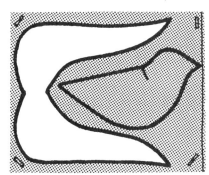

What You Need

bird pattern on page 25
scissors
pencil
construction paper
white glue
felt-tipped marking pen
stapler and staples

What You Do

1. Cut out the wing and body pattern pieces on page 25.

2. Trace the pattern onto one piece of construction paper.

3. Staple that piece of paper to another of the same color and cut two of each traced pattern shape.

4. Glue the two resulting wing shapes together and the two resulting body shapes together.

5. Cut a slit in the body and wings as shown.

6. Slide the wings into body slit and fold upward.

7. Spiral cut a tail *(optional)* from a square of construction paper.

8. Glue the tail onto the bird.

9. Using a felt-tipped marking pen, add eyes and a beak if desired.

10. Hang birds in clusters or from a wire circle made with a coat hanger.

Suggested Uses

Combine paper birds of different colors hung from strings of different lengths to create mobiles.

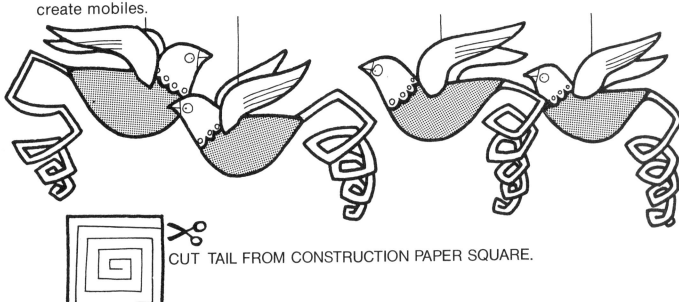

CUT TAIL FROM CONSTRUCTION PAPER SQUARE.

Paper Bird Pattern

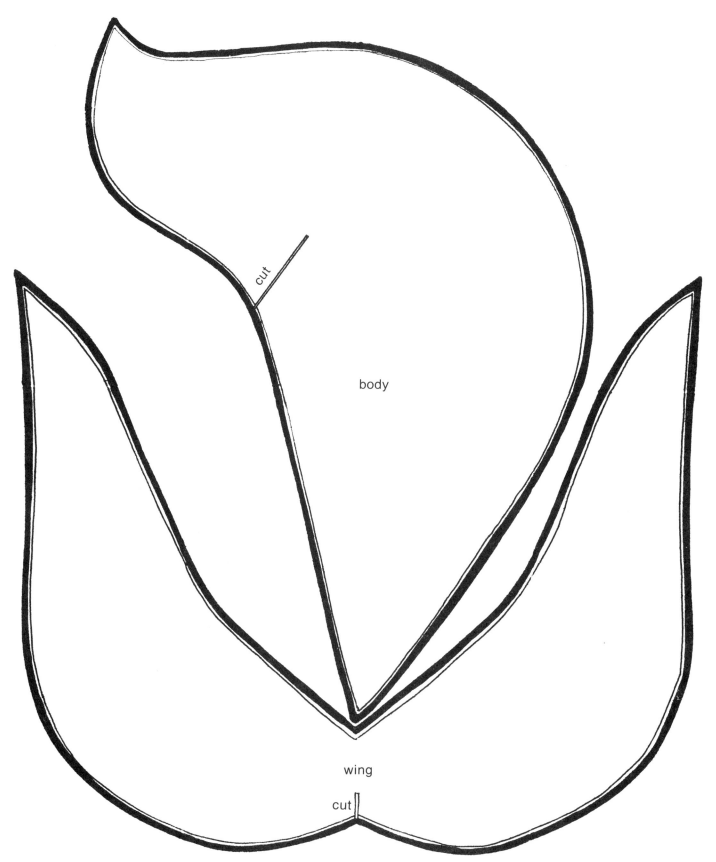

cut

body

wing

cut

Name _____

Basic Shapes and Random Gluing

What You Need

scissors
construction paper in assorted colors
glue

What You Do

1. Cut a basic shape from construction paper — perhaps a butterfly, a leaf, a tree, a circle, a square, or a triangle.

2. Cut small shapes about 1 to 2 inches in diameter at random from other colors of construction paper. Try using only three colors.

3. Glue the smaller shapes onto the larger basic shape. You may wish to do a repeated pattern, or to glue the pieces at random on the larger piece.

4. When you have finished your pattern, glue your work onto a separate piece of construction paper.

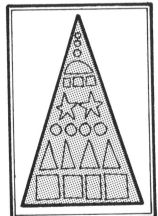

Name _____

Pop Art

What You Need

old magazines
scissors
white glue
construction paper

What You Do

1. From old magazines cut pictures of various people. Those pictures with bright, vivid colors work best.

2. Cut head, eyeglasses, hair, shirts, skirts, trousers, and shoes from a variety of pictures.

3. Arrange these various body parts into new "people." For example, combine the head of a tennis star with the body of a bathing suit model and the feet of a truck driver. Rearrange these parts until you are satisfied with your new person.

4. Glue all of the parts to a sheet of construction paper.

5. Write a brief description of this new person. What is his or her name? Where does he or she live? How does he or she spend free time?

Name _____

Special Eggs

What You Need

egg and chick patterns on page 29
one 6" x 8" piece of pastel (but *not* yellow) construction paper
one 6" x 6" piece of yellow construction paper
a third piece of construction paper in a complementary or contrasting color for the
    background
pencil
scissors
white glue
brad
felt-tipped marking pens

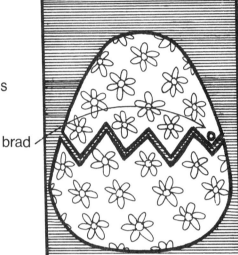

brad

What You Do

1. Using the pattern provided, draw an egg on a piece of pastel colored construction paper.

2. Cut out the egg.

3. In a zigzag motion, cut the egg into two pieces and save both.

4. Using the pattern provided, draw a chick on a piece of yellow construction paper.

5. Cut out the chick.

6. Glue the chick near the middle of the background sheet of construction paper.

7. Glue the bottom half of the egg to the background sheet of construction paper.

8. With a brad, fasten the top of the egg to one side of the glued bottom half so that the top and bottom touch. The top of the egg should remain loose so that it can be swung open and closed on the brad hinge.

9. Using marking pens, draw eyes and a beak on the chick.

10. Again using marking pens, decorate both the top and bottom halves of the egg with flowers, polka dots, stripes, or other patterns and motifs.

Suggestion

It may be easier to cut the egg and chick from folded paper.

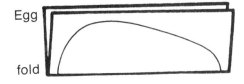

Egg

fold

Chick

fold

28

Name _____

Special Egg Patterns

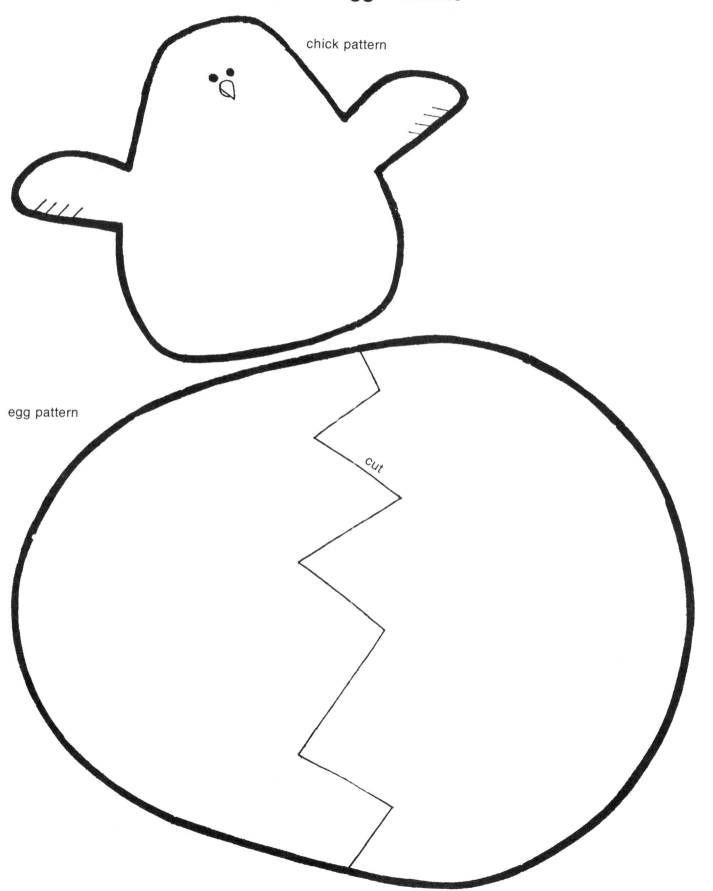

chick pattern

egg pattern

cut

Name _____

Marbled Paper — Floating Oil Method

What You Need

    white or light-colored butcher paper cut to size
    newspapers
    plastic tub *or* tote tray
    water
    oil paints (*not* acrylics) in three complementary colors
    three small, wide-mouthed jars to hold the paint
    turpentine
    pencil, popsicle stick, *or* tongue depressor
    heavy books *or* iron

What You Do

1. Cut large sheets of white or light-colored butcher paper to a size that will fit easily into the plastic tub or tray you plan to use.

2. Spread newspapers on your drying surface.

3. Fill the plastic tub with water to the depth of about 1 to 2 inches.

4. In separate containers, mix one teaspoon of each color of oil paint with just enough turpentine to thin it to pouring consistency.

5. Pour five or six drops of one color of paint over the water in the tub and swirl gently with a pencil, popsicle stick, or tongue depressor.

6. Repeat step 5 for each of the two remaining paint colors.

7. Lay one sheet of butcher paper over the oil floating on the surface of the water, quickly press out any air bubbles, and remove the paper. You should be able to see the colors from the back of the sheet as you press it onto the water's surface.

8. Lay the marbled paper out flat on newspaper, paint side up, to dry.

9. Once the paper dries, press it under heavy books or with a cool iron to flatten it.

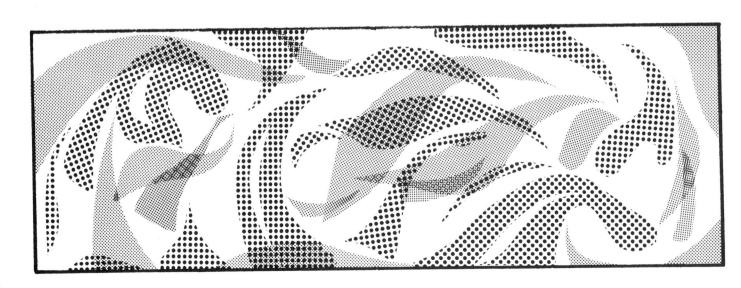

Name _____

Soap Balls or Crayons

What You Need

measuring cups and spoons
Ivory Snow Flakes
bowl
water
food coloring in assorted colors
gelatin molds
vegetable oil
dull knife

What You Do

1. To make soap balls, measure 1/4 cup of Ivory Snow Flakes into a bowl and add 1 tablespoon of water and one drop of food coloring. If you are making soap crayons, add ten drops of food coloring. Food coloring often comes only in the primary colors — red, yellow, and blue. If you want additional colors, remember that you can mix red and yellow to get orange, yellow and blue to get green, and blue and red to get purple.

2. Mix until all of the soap is evenly colored.

3. If you want scented soap, add perfume and mix again.

4. Using your hands, form the moistened soap flakes into balls or logs. Then, with a dull knife, cut the logs into shorter, crayon lengths. Or pack moistened soap into lightly greased gelatin molds.

5. Allow the soap to dry overnight.

6. If you make soap balls as a gift, wrap them in lightweight cloth, such as cheesecloth or nylon netting, and tie with ribbon or yarn.

Suggested Uses

Soap balls and crayons can be given as gifts. In addition, the crayons may be used for drawing (on paper or on porcelain bathtub sides and tile shower stall walls) and as floating bath and water time toys.

31

Name _____

Gonfalons (Banners)

What You Need

research materials on astrological signs or other symbol systems
9″ x 12″ pieces of felt in a variety of colors
pencil
scratch paper
straight pins
scissors
white glue
felt scraps in a variety of colors
cloth scraps in various solids, patterns, and prints
one stick or dowel 11 inches long
one piece of yarn 18 inches long

What You Do

1. Study astrological signs, symbols, and glyphs. For example, the name of one sign is Aries. The symbol for this sign is a ram, and the glyph for this sign looks like this ♈.

2. Select one piece of felt for the background.

3. On scratch paper, draw letters for your astrological name. Cut out these letters and use them as patterns.

4. Pin the paper letters onto a second color of felt and cut around them.

5. Glue the letters to the felt background.

6. Cut from felt and/or cloth scraps all of the other verbal and pictorial information you wish to add to your gonfalon. Consider including words or cutouts that represent your favorite sport, food, or activity.

7. When your gonfalon is complete, cut vertical slits at the top and weave a stick or dowel through these slits.

8. Tie one end of a piece of yarn to each end of the dowel. Use the yarn to hang the finished banner.

Suggested Variation

A **gonfalon** is a flag that hangs from a crosspiece or frame and often carries the symbol of a prince or a state. Make a larger banner to symbolize your family, school, neighborhood, town, city, state, country, or religious beliefs.

3-D Cards

What You Need

construction or stiff drawing paper
pencil
scissors
glue
crayons, pencils, pens, or paint for drawing and coloring

What You Do

1. Fold paper in half.

2. Draw one-half of a symmetrical shape along the folded edge, making certain to put tabs on the sides of the drawing. Leave at least a 1-inch margin all around your picture.

3. Cut along all lines except the ends of the tabs.

4. Unfold your picture, making sure it is still attached to the paper by the tabs on both sides.

5. Color your picture.

6. Push the picture out, away from the background. Crease the tabs.

7. To cover the space left by your cutout and to give the card a finished look, cut a second piece of paper the same size as the card. Fold this piece and glue the edges to the cutout card, making a cover.

8. Decorate the outside cover of your card.

Suggested Uses

Cards made in this way are perfect for expressing birthday and holiday greetings and other sentiments as well.

Name _____

Decorative Bottle

What You Need

old bottle or jar
tissue paper in assorted colors
scissors
liquid starch
shallow, wide-mouthed container (baby food jar or margarine tub)
two paintbrushes
clear shellac

What You Do

1. Remove the label from the bottle or jar.

2. Cut the tissue paper into small pieces.

3. Pour the starch into the container.

4. With one hand, hold a piece of tissue paper on the bottle. With the other hand, brush liquid starch over the tissue paper, onto the bottle. The starch will make the tissue stick to the bottle.

5. Repeat step 4, overlapping the pieces of tissue paper, until the bottle is completely covered.

6. Allow the starch to dry.

7. Using the other paintbrush, apply shellac to the bottle to make the surface shiny.

8. Allow the shellac to dry.

Suggested Uses

With this method, decorate containers for use as pencil holders, vases, and desk organizers.

Name _____

Cardboard and Scrap Collage

What You Need

old and used things (paper, cloth, yarn, wire, corks, etc.)
corrugated cardboard (about 9" x 12")
scissors
brown crayon
white glue
stapler and staples
18" piece of yarn or string

What You Do

1. Collect as many interesting things as you can (including bottle caps, thread, spools, etc.).

2. Cut the ends of the cardboard in a zigzag or other interesting pattern.

3. Cut a couple of holes in the cardboard for added interest.

4. Rub the side of a brown crayon across the cardboard to add color and texture.

5. Arrange your "found things" on the cardboard to make an interesting picture or design.

6. When you are satisfied with your design, glue each object in place.

7. Staple yarn or string to the back of the cardboard at the top right and left corners or edges.

8. Hang your collage for display.

Name _____

Stitchery Sampler

What You Need

burlap cut into 6″ x 6″ squares
masking tape
yarn
2″ large-eyed, blunt-tipped, plastic embroidery needle
scissors

What You Do

1. Tape edges of burlap to reinforce them and to keep the cloth from unraveling.

2. Design your own stitchery sampler using the stitches shown on page 37.

3. Add feathers or colorful weeds for texture.

4. Once you have mastered the basic stitches and made several squares, sew them together to make bell pulls, pillows, place mats, potholders, tapestries, and wall hangings.

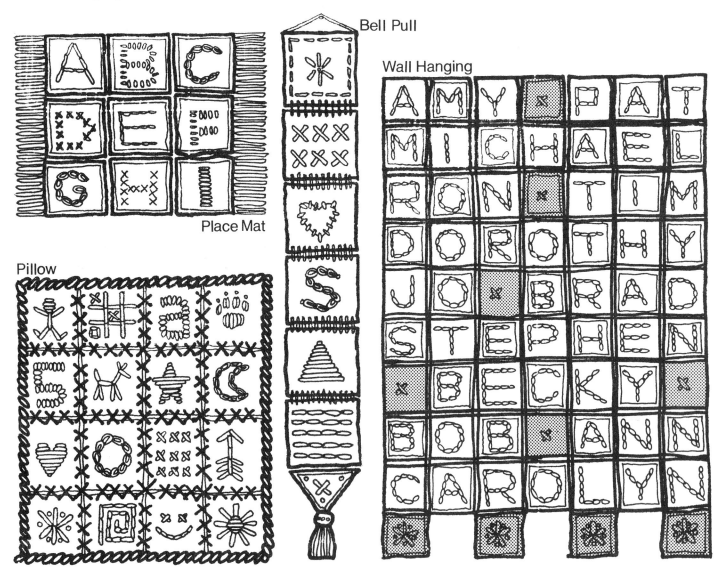

Place Mat

Bell Pull

Wall Hanging

Pillow

Name _____

Sample Stitches

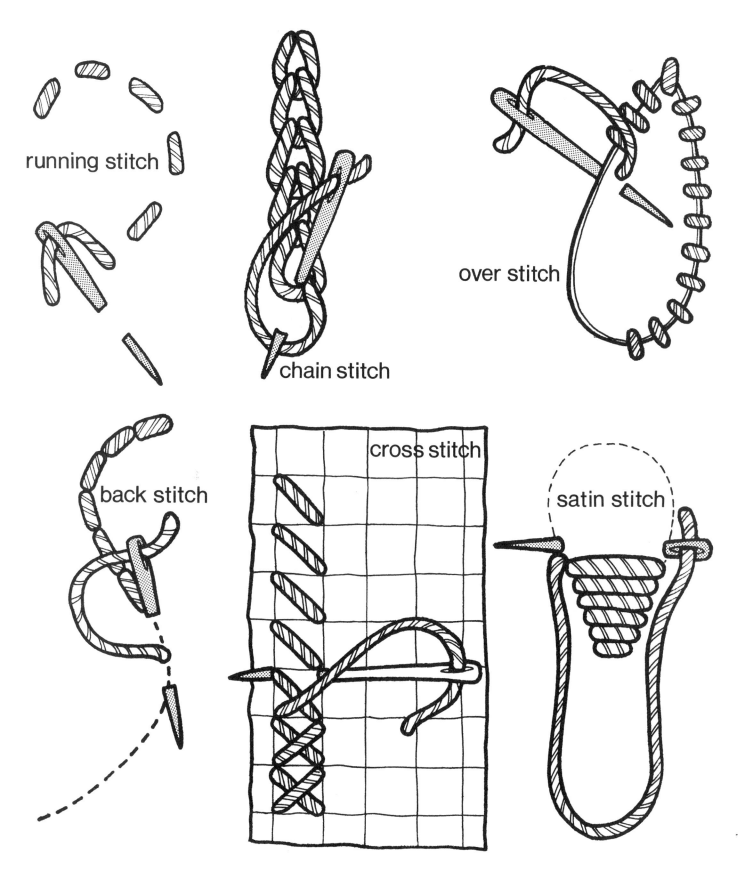

running stitch

chain stitch

over stitch

back stitch

cross stitch

satin stitch

Name _____

Construction Paper Rubbings

What You Need

    construction paper in assorted colors (9″ x 12″)
    scissors
    white glue
    one 9″ x 12″ sheet of white construction paper
    crayons
    one 12″ x 18″ sheet of construction paper

What You Do

1. Cut an animal or other shape from construction paper. Fish, birds, flowers, and trees with fruit and leaves make good shapes for this project.

2. Now cut repeating scallops, zigzags, or other strips and pieces from another color of construction paper. Glue these strips and pieces to your basic shape. As you add pieces of paper, you also add texture and depth.

3. When you are satisfied with the shape and texture of your artwork, place a sheet of white construction paper over it. With the flat surface of a crayon, rub over the design and watch the pattern appear.

4. Glue both the original cut design and the rubbing onto a single sheet of construction paper.

5. Display your artwork on a bulletin board or wall.

 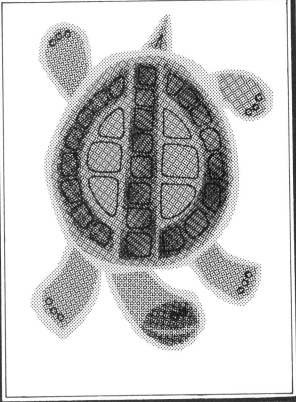

Name _____

Aluminum Foil Stained Glass

What You Need

cardboard (cut to 8" x 8")
white glue
yarn or string of medium thickness
aluminum foil
masking tape
permanent felt-tipped marking pens in black and assorted colors

What You Do

1. "Draw" a design on the cardboard with white glue.

2. Lay yarn or string on the glue and press it down firmly.

3. Cover the cardboard and string with aluminum foil. Turn the cardboard over and secure the foil with masking tape.

4. Press the foil down in the spaces created by the string pattern.

5. Use *permanent* felt-tipped marking pens (water-based pens will *not* work) to color in all of the low spaces.

6. Use a *permanent* black felt-tipped marking pen to outline the raised areas.

Name _____

Nature's Window

What You Need

    two pieces of wax paper (9″ x 12″)
    scissors
    dried leaves and flowers (pressed)
    scraps of colored tissue paper
    white glue
    newspapers
    iron
    two construction paper strips (2″ x 9″)
    stapler and staples
    hole punch
    one 18″ piece of string or yarn

What You Do

1. Cut two pieces of wax paper exactly the same size (9″ x 12″).

2. On one piece of the wax paper, arrange dried leaves, dried pressed flower petals, and pieces of tissue paper, then glue these items in place on the wax paper.

3. Place your design on top of several newspapers, design side up. Lay the second sheet of wax paper over it.

4. With the iron set on **low**, iron over the wax paper, moving the iron from the center outward. The two pieces of wax paper will melt together.

5. Cut two strips of construction paper each 2 inches wide and 9 inches long.

6. Fold the construction paper strips in half and staple them to the wax paper, one at the top and one at the bottom.

7. Punch a hole near each top corner. Insert one end of the string or yarn through each hole and tie.

8. Hang your window so that light passes through it.

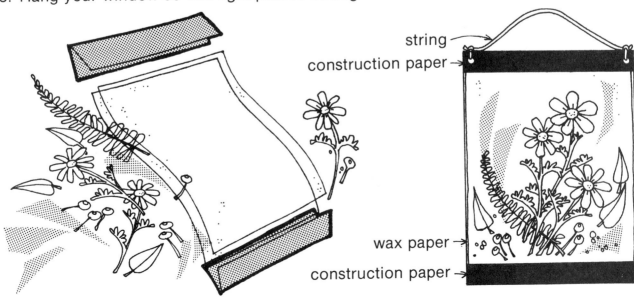

string
construction paper
wax paper
construction paper

Name _____

Scrap Wood - Tape Designs

What You Need

scraps of ½″ plywood
clear contact paper
broad-tipped marking pens *or* tempera paints in various colors
masking or electricians' tape

What You Do

1. Clean your scrap wood of any dirt or splinters.

2. Cut contact paper to create a design.

3. Peel the backing off the contact paper and place it, sticky side down, onto the wood.

4. When the design is in place, use pens or paints to color in between the paper pieces and strips.

5. Peel off the contact paper. Then use a black felt-tipped pen to outline the areas formerly covered by it.

6. Color the four edges of the wood to complete the project.

Variations

Use masking or electricians' tape instead of contact paper, but *press it down firmly* to seal it to the wood so that your ink or paint will not "bleed" under it.

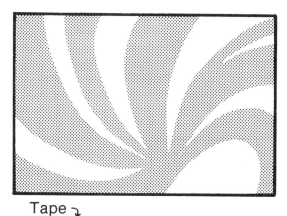

Contact paper applied to wood

Tape

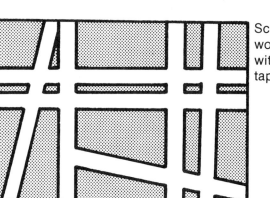

Scrap wood with tape

Name _____

String Dolls

What You Need

one 6″ x 12″ piece of cardboard
scissors
ruler
pencil
sheet of newspaper
40 to 50 yards of string
white glue
two buttons
felt and yarn scraps

What You Do

1. Cut out a square slot in the top of your cardboard for the head. Then measure down 8 inches, mark with your pencil, and cut out a longer and thinner slot for the body.

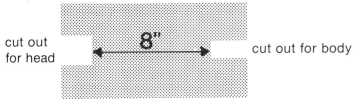

cut out for head   **8″**   cut out for body

2. Crumple up one half sheet of newspaper to form a ball for the head, and wrap string tightly around this ball until it is completely covered.

3. Insert the head into the square slot of the cardboard. Then wrap string around the head and down through the bottom slot about 75 to 100 times.

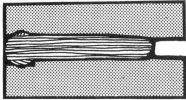

4. Cut through all layers of string at the bottom of the slot and carefully remove the cardboard frame.

5. Tie a piece of string around the head so that all of the string on the head will stay in place. Then tie a piece of string around the neck.

6. Separate several strands of string for the arms and tie off for the wrists. Then trim excess string for hands.

7. Tie a piece of string around the waist. Separate the rest of the string in half for legs and tie at the ankles.

8. Glue on buttons for eyes, felt scraps for facial features, and yarn for hair.

9. Dress and finish the doll in whatever way you like. For example, you might add an apron, bow tie, hair bow, hat, or cap.

Name _____

White Glue Rubbings

What You Need

one 9″ x 12″ piece of black construction paper
white glue
one 9″ x 12″ piece of white construction paper
crayons
colored chalk
two pieces of construction paper at least 11″ x 14″ to be used for mounting and "framing"

What You Do

1. Think of a simple shape or design.

2. Using white glue, "draw" the design or picture you have in mind on a sheet of black construction paper.

3. Allow the glue to dry completely.

4. Lay the white sheet of construction paper over the black sheet. Rub the side of a crayon over the design so that the design is transferred onto the white paper.

5. Using crayons of different colors, fill in the design as you wish.

6. Using colored chalk, fill in the glue design you drew on black paper. Press heavily so that the colored chalk will show up on the black paper.

7. Mount the white crayon transfer and the black glue picture each on a larger piece of construction paper.

8. Display your white glue drawing and your crayon rubbing side by side.

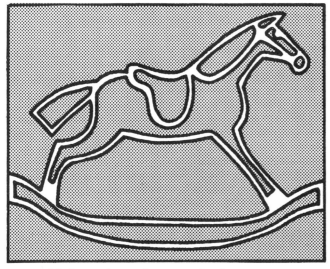

Using glue, draw a design on black paper. Then color in the design with colored chalk.

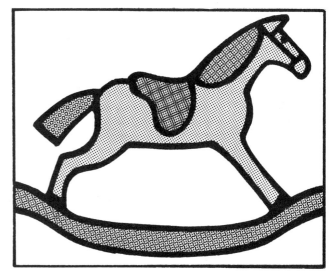

Rub white paper with broad side of crayon to transfer glue design.

Name _____

Cup Towers

What You Need

four to eight styrofoam cups
x-acto knife
white glue
tempera paints
paintbrush

What You Do

1. Using an x-acto knife, cut openings in four to eight cups to create a lacy effect.

2. Stack and glue the cups to make a tower.

3. Paint your tower with tempera paints if you wish.

Name _____

String Paintings

What You Need

string
scissors
tempera paints
shallow, wide-mouthed containers
paintbrush
one 12" x 18" piece of light-colored construction paper
felt-tipped marking pens

What You Do

1. Cut several pieces of string approximately 8 inches long.

2. Pour paints into shallow containers.

3. Dip each string into one color of paint. Take the string out of the paint, and remove the excess paint with a paintbrush.

4. Lay the "painted string" on one side of the construction paper. Then fold the other side of the construction paper onto the string.

5. Hold the folded side of the construction paper down firmly as you pull the string from between both sides of the folded paper.

6. Repeat steps 3, 4, and 5 several times, using a new piece of string and a different color of paint each time.

7. Lay your string painting out flat and allow it to dry.

Variation

Outline some areas of the design with felt-tipped marking pens.

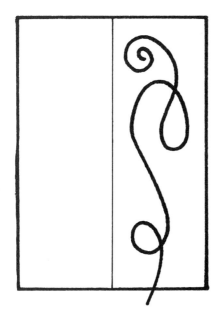 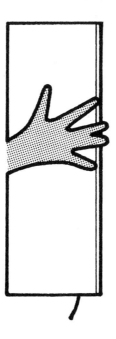 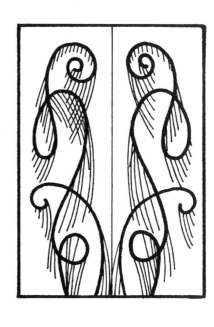

Name _____

Magic Marker Fabric Design

What You Need

white cloth (100 percent cotton, polyester blend, sharkstooth, or muslin) cut to size desired for group project

permanent felt-tipped marking pens in assorted colors and with tips of varying widths

newspaper *or* butcher paper

thumb tacks *or* masking tape

What You Do

1. Divide the cloth into sections. Use a black, felt-tipped *permanent* marking pen to outline these sections. Then assign each participating artist a section.

2. Spread newspapers or butcher paper on a large table or other work surface.

3. Tack or tape the cloth securely to the table and indicate the position of the top and bottom.

4. Encourage each participant to draw a design or create a picture inside his or her assigned section.

5. When all of the sections have been filled with individual pictures or designs, remove the cloth from the table.

Suggested Uses

Use the decorated fabric as a banner, tablecloth, or wall hanging, or to make a shirt or skirt. Banners might be used to advertise carnivals, festivals, or book and film fairs. Shirts or skirts might be worn for open house or on the last day of school. Colors will not run or fade when the cloth is washed if *permanent* markers are used.

46

Name _____

Drawn Burlap

What You Need

one 8″ x 12″ piece of burlap
thread and yarn of various colors and textures
2″ large-eye plastic embroidery needle
scissors
found objects *(optional)*
10″ x ¼″ dowel
white glue

What You Do

1. Pull some of the *horizontal* strings out of the cloth. Remove them one at a time to "open up" areas for weaving. Experiment with the spacing between the remaining strings.

2. Weave or embroider with thread or yarn of a variety of colors and textures.

3. Add found objects if desired.

4. Weave a dowel through the top of the burlap approximately 1½ inches from the top edge.

5. Tie the ends of an 18-inch piece of yarn to the ends of the dowel.

6. Turn the completed piece over and apply a thin bead of white glue around all four edges to keep the remaining strings from unraveling or pulling through.

7. Allow glue to dry completely before hanging.

Suggested Uses

Use this technique to make place mats, wall hangings, and window decorations.

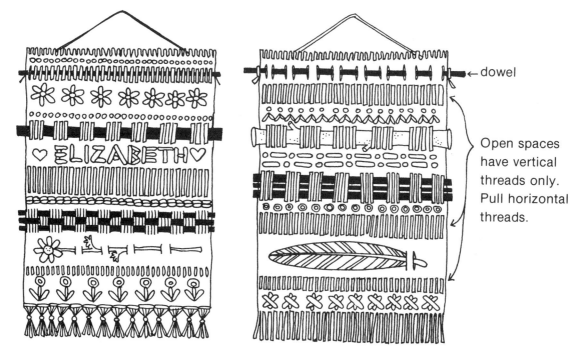

←dowel

Open spaces have vertical threads only. Pull horizontal threads.

Name _____

Crayon Batik

What You Need

pencil
paper
one 10″ x 15″ piece of *cotton* cloth
    (Use sheeting or muslin; polyester
    does not accept wax.)
newspapers
thumb tacks *or* masking tape
liquid dye
plastic washtub *or* 3-pound coffee can
electric frying pan lined with alumi-
    num foil

broken crayons with paper removed
paraffin
one 6-cup muffin tin
six tongue depressors or popsicle
    sticks
one 1″ bristle paintbrush for each color
    of wax
rubber gloves
stick *or* paint stirrer
sink and running water
iron
permanent, black, felt-tipped marking
    pen

What You Do

1. With a pencil and/or crayons, create a picture or design on paper.

2. Lightly pencil your design onto your piece of cloth.

3. Spread newspapers over your entire work area.

4. Lay your piece of cloth over a stack of newspapers and tack or tape it to your work surface.

5. Prepare the dye in a washtub or can according to the directions on the package.

6. Turn on the frying pan and set the heat control knob on 350°.

7. Put broken crayons in individual muffin cups with one or two 1-inch squares of paraffin, and set the muffin tin in the frying pan.

8. Using one tongue depressor or popsicle stick for each color, stir the crayon wax and paraffin to blend. The resulting mixture should be the consistency of cream. Add additional crayons and small amounts of paraffin as needed to maintain desired amount and consistency.

9. Using a separate brush for each color, paint your design in wax on the cloth.

Name_____

Crayon Batik

(continued)

10. When the wax is cool and hard, crumple the cloth slightly so that the wax coating cracks.

11. Put on the rubber gloves.

12. Dip the cloth into the dye. Using the stick or paint stirrer, stir the cloth gently in the dye until it is entirely submerged, then let it stand for approximately four minutes.

13. Using the stick again, lift the cloth from the dye.

14. With your gloved hands, carefully squeeze the excess moisture from the cloth back into the washtub or can.

15. Rinse the cloth at the sink under cold running water. Squeeze the excess water and dye from the cloth.

16. Hang the cloth from a line or over a wire fence or tree limb until dry.

17. Lay the dried cloth *between* four or five sheets of newspaper. With the iron set on **cotton**, iron the newspapers. When the newspapers become waxy, replace them with fresh newspapers and repeat the ironing process until all of the wax has been absorbed from the cloth.

18. *(Optional)* Using a *permanent*, black, felt-tipped marking pen, outline the finished design to enhance the batik pattern.

19. Hang the finished batik near lights or windows for best results.

Suggested Uses

Use the batik technique to create clothing, tablecloths, pictures, or wall hangings.

Name _____

Tissue Paper Rubbings

What You Need

objects to be rubbed
scraps of colored tissue paper
black crayon with paper removed
scissors
aluminum foil
one 9" x 12" piece of cardboard or tagboard
masking tape
two paintbrushes
white glue
clear shellac
stapler and staples
string

What You Do

1. Find objects that have textured surfaces or raised patterns (window screening, cement, rocks, leaves, bark, etc.).

2. Place a piece of colored tissue paper over the object, then rub the side of the crayon over the paper.

3. Trim the tissue paper in any shape you want.

4. Fold a piece of aluminum foil around the cardboard or tagboard, and secure it on the back with pieces of tape.

5. Arrange your rubbings on the foil in an interesting pattern.

6. Brush watered-down white glue onto the foil surface. Glue the tissue rubbings to the foil, overlapping colors for added interest.

7. Allow the glue to dry.

8. Using a different paintbrush, apply a coat of clear shellac to the entire surface and allow to dry overnight.

9. Staple a small piece of string to the back of the cardboard for a hanger.

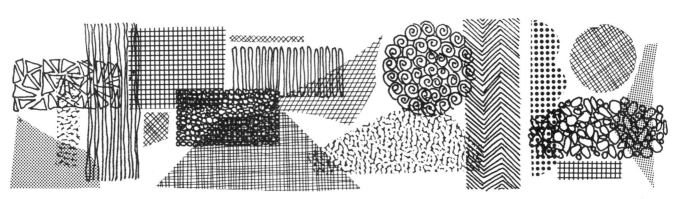

Huichol Yarn Painting

Background Information

The Huichols are an Indian tribe of central Mexico. While no one knows exactly where they originated, theories abound. Their language suggests a relationship with the ancient Aztecs. Other evidence suggests they came from coastal Mexico and migrated eastward. Regardless of their origins, they have traditionally lived in scattered settlements and led seminomadic lives.

To primitive man, all sacred things are symbols; and the Huichols are a primitive people. For them, religion is a personal matter, not an institutional one. Their lives are religious, wrapped in symbolism from cradle to grave.[1]

It is in this religious context and in this symbolic language that the Huichols create their art. "For the Huichol, art is prayer and direct communication with and participation in the sacred realm. It is meant to assure the good and beautiful life: health and fertility of crops, animals, and people; prosperity of the individual, the kin group, and the larger society. Art, then, is functional as well as beautiful."[2]

One form Huichol art takes is yarn painting. To create this unique form, the Huichols cover a board with beeswax. Then they scratch a design into the wax and carefully press yarn into the scratched design. Huichol artists work with one color at a time to portray a single shape or object, developing with the yarn a pattern that emphasizes the characteristic feel and texture of the object. The resulting art form has been widely studied and copied throughout the Western world.

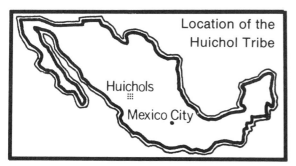

Location of the
Huichol Tribe

Huichols

Mexico City

[1] Carl Lumholtz, *Symbolism of the Huichol Indians*, Memoirs of the American Museum of Natural History (New York, 1900).

[2] *Art of the Huichol Indians,* edited by Kathleen Berrin (New York: Fine Arts Museums of San Francisco/Harry N. Abrams, Inc., 1978).

Name _____

Huichol Yarn Painting

What You Need

pencil
one 9″ x 12″ piece of cardboard or railroad board
permanent, black, felt-tipped marking pen
paintbrush
white glue
scissors
nylon yarn in a variety of bright colors
bias tape *or* ribbon in a matching or complementary color

What You Do

1. With the pencil, draw a design composed of open, simple shapes on your board.

2. When you are satisfied with the design, outline it with the marking pen.

3. Brush a small amount of glue evenly over the surface of the board. The lines of your design should be visible through the glue.

4. Wash and wipe your hands.

5. Select several colors of yarn and cut pieces in manageable lengths. For each shape, use a single shade of yarn or several shades of the same color.

6. Slowly lay the yarn onto the glued surface, following the lines of your design as closely as possible. Using your pencil point, push the yarn into place and press it against the board. Lay the pieces of yarn as close together as possible. Work slowly and wipe the glue from your fingers and the board as you go along.

7. Continuing to work in this manner, cover the entire board with yarn, whether as part of the design or background.

8. Trim away excess yarn and, where possible, tuck under loose ends.

9. Allow yarn and board to dry.

10. To finish the edges and create a border, braid several shades of yarn of the same colors as those used in your painting. Make this braid at least 42 inches long, and glue it around the edge. Or glue one edge of bias tape or ribbon to the board front, mitering the corners as needed, and the other edge to the board back.

Additional References

National Geographic, June 1977.

Prieto, Mariana, and Grizella Hopper. *Bridmen of Papantla.* Paintings by McDuff Everton. Pasadena, Calif.: Ward Ritchie Press.

Name _____

String Ball

What You Need

    one small balloon
    one large ball of string
    scissors
    ruler
    white glue
    old lunch bag
    felt or construction paper scraps
    pipe cleaner

What You Do

1. Blow up the balloon until it is firm. Knot the open end.

2. Tie a piece of string to the knot and suspend the balloon from something (the back of a chair, for instance) so that it hangs free and does *not* rest on or against any surface.

3. Cut the rest of the string into 20-inch lengths.

4. Squeeze some glue onto a flattened lunch bag.

5. Dip a piece of string in the glue. Holding and pulling with the fingers of one hand, run the string lightly between the thumb and index finger of your other hand to distribute the glue evenly and remove the excess.

6. Wrap the glue-coated string around the balloon from the bottom to the top, *overlapping* the string near the knot in the balloon but making certain not to cover it.

7. Allow the string to dry for 30 minutes.

8. Continue wrapping the balloon with string, criss-crossing as you wrap.

9. Again, allow the string to dry for 30 minutes.

10. Add more string, wrapping in different directions, until the balloon is completely covered.

11. Once again, allow the string to dry for 30 minutes.

12. Cut the string from which the balloon is hanging.

13. With a straight pin or scissors point, pop the balloon and deflate it.

14. Holding the knotted end of the balloon, gently pull it through the hole left open when you layered string around the knot (see step 6).

Name _____

String Ball

(continued)

15. Decorate the string ball by gluing felt or construction paper scraps to its surface to make a face or a design.

16. Fashion a hanger by inserting a pipe cleaner in the string ball near the top where the knot was. Bend and/or twist the pipe cleaner as needed to shape and attach it.

Suggested Uses

Using this technique, create clown faces, globes, jack-o'-lanterns, or holiday ornaments.

Name _____

Colored Chalk and Fabric

What You Need

plastic sheet *or* tablecloth
water
newspapers
old cotton sheets or unbleached muslin
colored chalks
iron
wax paper

What You Do

1. Cover your table or work surface with a plastic sheet or tablecloth.

2. Thoroughly moisten a pad of newspapers and lay it on the plastic-covered surface.

3. Completely saturate the cloth with water and place it on the moistened newspapers.

4. Using chalk, draw pictures or designs on the cloth. Apply the chalk freely and heavily for bright colors and vivid images. The chalk will return to its original color value when it dries.

5. Hang the cloth from a line or limb and allow it to dry thoroughly.

6. Lay the dry cloth on a padded ironing board or on a pad of *dry* newspapers.

7. Place a sheet of wax paper over the cloth.

8. With the iron set on **cotton**, press the wax paper over the cloth. Doing so will deepen the colors and fix the chalk so it will not rub off.

9. Hang the finished cloth on a wall or in a window.

Name _____

Pastels and India Ink

What You Need

oil base pastels
one 7½"x 10" piece of dark-colored construction paper (green, blue, purple, or black)
black India ink
paintbrush
white glue
one 9" x 12" piece of light-colored construction paper

What You Do

1. Think of a theme: birds, butterflies, fish, flowers, or leaves.

2. Using pastels, draw and then color a large bird, butterfly, fish, flower, or leaf on the dark paper. Use bright colors and fill in the design completely.

3. Brush India ink over your design.

4. Allow the ink to dry.

5. Glue your design to the larger, light-colored sheet of construction paper so this sheet forms both a backing and a frame for your art.

Things to Think About

What happened when you applied the ink over the pastels?

What effect would you get if you used light-colored paper rather than dark?

What changes would you make in your design if you used this technique a second time?

Name _____

Rough Paper Watercoloring

What You Need

pencil
one piece of white drawing paper
textured surfaces, such as metal screen, plastered wall, cement, or concrete
white crayon with paper removed
watercolors
paintbrush
fine-tipped marking pens in dark colors
white glue
one sheet of colored construction paper

What You Do

1. Using a pencil, lightly sketch a simple picture or design on a piece of drawing paper.

2. Select a textured surface, and lay the drawing paper over it.

3. Holding the paper firmly in place with one hand, rub the side of a white crayon back and forth across it with the other hand.

4. Paint a design in bright watercolors on the crayon-waxed paper. The wax will resist the watercolor.

5. Allow the paint to dry.

6. Using the marking pens, outline portions of your work to enhance the colors.

7. Glue your watercolor to the construction paper so that the latter forms both a backing and a frame for your work.

Name _____

Roll-on Paintings

What You Need

    pliers
    three or more empty roll-on deodorant containers
    liquid tempera paints
    liquid soap
    water
    newsprint *or* watercolor paper

What You Do

1. Collect several empty roll-on deodorant containers.

2. With pliers, gently but firmly snap off the caps of these containers, being careful *not* to crack or break the cap or the container.

3. Wash and rinse the containers thoroughly, stand them to drain, and allow them to dry.

4. Fill each container with a mixture of tempera paint, a few drops of liquid soap, and a small amount of water. The resulting mixture should be the consistency of cream. Replace the cap.

5. Continue filling the containers, putting one color in each, until you have filled them all. Be sure you have at least one red, one yellow, and one blue.

6. Using your imagination, create designs, textures, repeating patterns, and realistic pictures by rolling paint onto newsprint or watercolor paper. Overlap the colors and patterns.

7. When the paint in one container has been used up, refill the container following the procedure described in step 4.

8. Store the containers with original screw-on caps in place.

Name _____

Glue Designs with Watercolor

What You Need

white watercolor or drawing paper
white glue
watercolors
paintbrush
water
container for water
acrylic gloss *(optional)*
colored construction paper

What You Do

1. Draw a design by trailing a line of glue directly onto your white paper.
2. Allow the glue to dry.
3. When the glue has become transparent, brush bright watercolor washes over the paper. Use little water and lots of color because strong color is most effective.
4. Allow the paint to dry.
5. Brush a coat of acrylic gloss *(optional)* over your work to add more luster.
6. Glue your work to a piece of colored construction paper large enough to provide both a backing and a frame.

Variation

Use liquid tempera paints instead of watercolors.

Name _____

Painted Dots with Q-Tips

Pointillism is the technique of painting by applying dots or tiny strokes of pure color to a surface. Seen from a distance, these dots blend to create shades and values and to portray the play of light itself. Georges Seurat (1859-1891), a French artist, was a master of this technique. You can experiment with it using liquid tempera paints and Q-tips.

What You Need

white drawing paper
pencil
Q-tips
liquid tempera paints
paper towels
white glue
colored construction paper

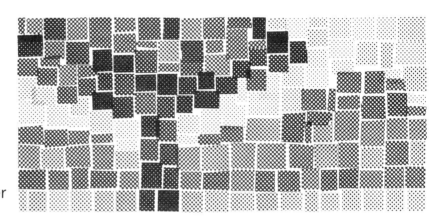

What You Do

1. Sketch a scene, a design, or a single shape, such as that of a leaf, a circle, or a butterfly.
2. Decide what color or colors you wish to use to fill in each space within your picture.
3. Dip one end of a Q-tip into paint. Blot the Q-tip on paper towels to remove the excess paint. Then make colored dots where you decided that color was needed. Place your dots as close together as you can with just a little white paper showing between them.
4. Using a different Q-tip for each color of paint, fill in the other areas of your picture. As you work, notice the effect of putting one color next to another. For example, what is the effect of filling in an area with an equal number of scattered yellow and blue dots? What happens when one area is filled entirely with red dots and the area next to it is filled entirely with green dots? What effect does this have on both colors?
5. Allow the paint to dry.
6. Glue your pointillist painting to a piece of construction paper cut large enough to provide both a backing and a frame for your artwork.

Variation

Vary the size of the dots by using toothpicks instead of Q-tips. Notice that the effect achieved by using smaller dots is totally different.

Name _____

Sponge Painting on Basic Shapes

What You Need

newspapers
paper towels
tempera paints
one 6-cup muffin tin *or* other similar container for paints
scissors
white construction paper
water
shallow, wide-mouthed container for water
small sponge pieces
white glue
colored construction paper

What You Do

1. Spread several layers of newspapers or paper towels over your work surface.
2. Pour one color of paint into each cup of the muffin tin. *Or* fill only three cups with color and use remaining cups to hold corresponding sponge pieces.
3. Cut a simple shape from white construction paper.
4. Dip a sponge piece into water and squeeze out the excess moisture.
5. Dip the water-softened sponge piece into one color of paint, press the sponge against the side of the paint container to remove excess paint or blot it on paper towels, then print onto the cutout shape.
6. Repeat step 5, using a different sponge piece for each paint color. Working in this manner, create a border for your shape or fill it in entirely.
7. Allow the paint to dry.
8. Glue the shape to a sheet of construction paper.

Variations

Limit your painting to only two or three colors.
Use several colors and overlap them as you print.

Name _____

Flooded Color

What You Need

newspapers
paper towels
shallow plastic tub *or* tote tray
water
watercolor or drawing paper
tempera paints
paintbrushes
felt-tipped marking pens
white glue
colored construction paper

What You Do

1. Spread several layers of newspapers or paper towels over your work surface.
2. Put about 2 inches of water in the plastic tub.
3. Dip the watercolor or drawing paper into the water and agitate or wiggle it to saturate it thoroughly.
4. Lay the saturated paper on your paper-covered work surface. Smooth it with your fingertips if necessary.
5. Paint directly on the saturated paper, letting the paint blend and run together. Use different colors. Experiment by dropping tiny drops of color onto the wet paper.
6. Allow the paint to dry.
7. Use felt-tipped marking pens to add outlines or details.
8. Glue your painting to a piece of colored construction paper cut large enough to form both a frame and a backing for your artwork.
9. Display your painting on a bulletin board or wall.

Name _____

Fluorescent Paint Design

What You Need

one 12" x 18" piece of white construction paper
fluorescent paint in assorted colors
watercolor paintbrushes
scissors
brass brads
one piece of colored construction paper cut to approximately 11" x 14"
white glue

What You Do

1. Paint diagonal stripes of varying colors and widths on white construction paper.
2. Allow the paint to dry.
3. Fold your paper in half so that each half measures 9 inches by 12 inches.
4. Cut your paper in half along the fold line.
5. Cut shapes from one piece of painted paper.
6. Glue the cutout pieces onto the uncut piece of painted paper to create a design of opposing stripes and angles.
7. Use brads to attach circles and create a moving design.
8. Glue your finished artwork to construction paper of a complementary color.

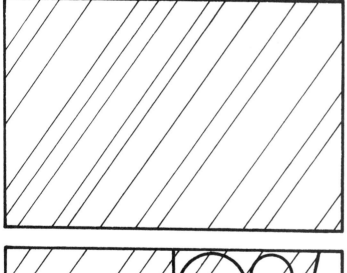

brads

Name _____

Painting with Q-Tips and Liquid Bleach

What You Need

liquid bleach
baby food jar *or* other small, wide-mouthed glass container
Q-tip
one 9" x 12" piece of dark-colored construction paper
felt-tipped marking pens
white glue
one 11" x 14" piece of construction paper in a contrasting color

What You Do

1. Pour a small amount of liquid bleach into the glass container.
2. Dip the Q-tip into the bleach and then use it to draw a scene, design, or pattern on the dark construction paper.
3. Allow the bleach to dry.
4. Use felt-tipped marking pens to outline or enhance parts of your artwork.
5. Glue your artwork to a slightly larger piece of construction paper in a contrasting color.

> **Caution**
>
> Bleach will lighten or remove color from fabric and will irritate skin and eyes. Avoid splashing or splattering it, and wash your hands thoroughly when you have finished this project. Should you get bleach on your skin or in your eyes, flush immediately and repeatedly with cold water.

Name _____

Coffee Filter Snowflakes

What You Need

#4 or #6 Melitta coffee filters
scissors
watercolors *or* colored inks (*not* tempera paints)
paintbrush
rimmed plate *or* traylike container to hold paint or ink
black construction paper
white glue

What You Do

1. Cut the perforated edge off the filter.
2. Fold the filter as shown.
3. Cut patterns in the folded edges, but leave portions of these edges uncut.
4. Dip the folded and cut edges of the filter into watercolor or ink, and hold them there until the filter has absorbed the liquid.
5. Unfold the filter snowflake and allow it to dry flat.
6. Hang the filter snowflake in a window or glue it to a piece of black construction paper.

Variation

Using a brush, paint the filter with watercolors as you unfold each section. Doing so will yield snowflakes of brighter colors.

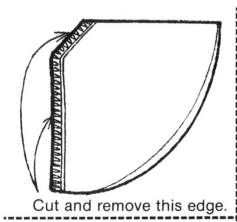

Cut and remove this edge.

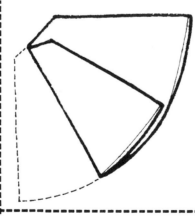

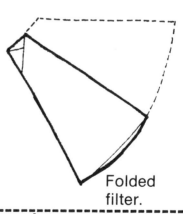

Folded filter.

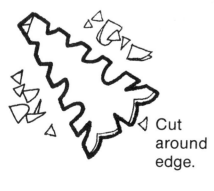

Cut around edge.

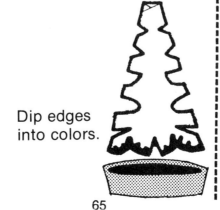

Dip edges into colors.

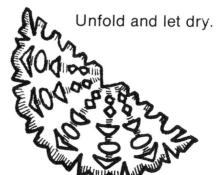

Unfold and let dry.

Name _____

Hand Print Bugs and Monsters

What You Need

tempera paints in assorted colors
paintbrushes
newsprint
paper towels *or* old rags
felt-tipped marking pens *or* crayons

What You Do

1. Paint the palm of one hand and the undersides of the fingers on that same hand with one color of tempera paint.
2. Press your painted hand firmly onto the paper so that it leaves a hand print.
3. Wipe your hand clean on paper towels or old rags.
4. Paint your other hand using the same color or a different one.
5. Press your painted hand onto the paper, touching the first print but not completely covering it.
6. Complete your creature by using crayons or felt-tipped marking pens to add nose, eyes, ears, teeth, legs, tails, or feet.
7. Name your creature.

THE FRIGHTFULLY FEARSOME FOUR-HORNED FINGERLEG

Name _____

Brayer Prints

What You Need

    water soluble inks in several colors
    one piece of plate glass
    newsprint, construction paper, *or* butcher paper
    brayer
    white glue
    construction paper in a contrasting color

What You Do

1. Put a small amount of ink on the glass.
2. With the brayer, spread the ink evenly over the surface of the glass.
3. Roll the inked flat surface, edge, or end of the brayer over the paper.
4. Wash the brayer and glass.
5. Repeat steps 1, 2, 3, and 4 using different colors of ink until your print is complete.
6. Allow your print to dry.
7. Glue your print onto a larger sheet of construction paper of a contrasting color.

Variations

Experiment with different colors of ink and with different rolling objects (for example, coin edges, rolling pins, and toy wheels).

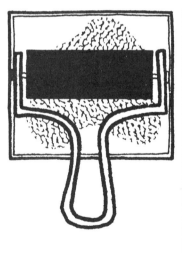
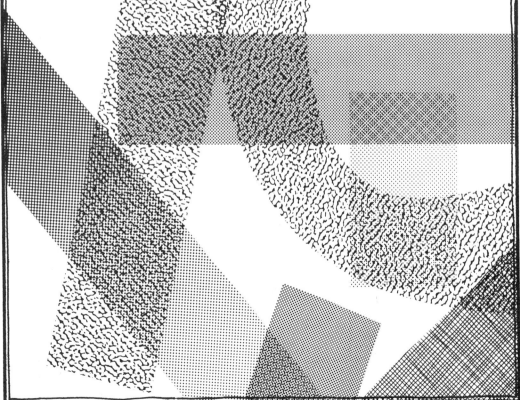

Name _____

Spatter Prints

What You Need

leaves *or* similar simple shapes cut from construction paper
shoe box
ruler
white construction paper
scissors
straight pins
masking tape
tagboard *or* cardboard
screen
old toothbrush
colored inks *or* tempera paints
paper towels
fine, felt-tipped marking pens
white glue
construction paper of a contrasting color

What You Do

1. Collect leaves or cut similar simple pattern shapes from construction paper.
2. Measure the inside of your shoe box and cut the white construction paper to fit easily into this space.
3. Lay the paper in the box.
4. Pin the leaves or shapes onto the paper.
5. Put a strip of tape over one edge of the screen or tape a strip of cardboard securely to the screen to serve as a handle.
6. Hold the screen over the open box with one hand. (The screen should be at least one inch above the paper.)
7. With your other hand, dip the toothbrush into ink or paint and blot in on a paper towel.
8. Rub the ink- or paint-filled brush over the screen, allowing a fine mist of color to fall on the paper below.
9. Remove the screen and then the pins and pattern shapes.
10. Allow the ink or paint to dry for at least one hour.
11. *(Optional)* Using felt-tipped marking pens, add any outlines you feel are needed.
12. Glue your spatter print to a piece of construction paper that is just enough larger than your print to form both a backing and a frame.

Variation

Use dark construction paper, such as blue or black, and white or light-colored ink or paint.

Suggested Uses

Use this technique to produce greeting cards, wrapping paper, or background sheets for other art.

Name _____

Tempera Printing

What You Need

textured items, such as fruits, leaves, vegetables, spools, rocks, and papers
small paring knife
x-acto knife
newspaper
newsprint, butcher or shelf paper, *or* construction paper
paint cups
liquid tempera paint in assorted colors
one paintbrush for each color

What You Do

1. Collect some textured items, such as fruits, leaves, vegetables, spools, rocks, and papers.
2. If you are using fruits or vegetables, cut them in half to produce a flat surface with which you can print. If you are using a potato, cut it in half, draw a shape on one of the flat surfaces, and then cut away the potato around the shape so that the shape stands out.
3. Cover your work surface with newspapers.
4. Fill the paint cups with tempera paint.
5. Dip the object with which you are printing directly into the paint or use a brush to coat the flat side of the object with paint.
6. Press the object, painted side down, onto your paper.
7. Repeat steps 5 and 6 as many times as are needed to fill your paper with a repeating design. Wash the excess paint from the object you are using and try another color or select a different object to use with the same or a different color. Try overlapping patterns and colors.
8. Continue until your design is complete.
9. Allow the paint to dry.

Suggested Uses

Use this technique to create greeting cards, note paper, and wrapping paper.

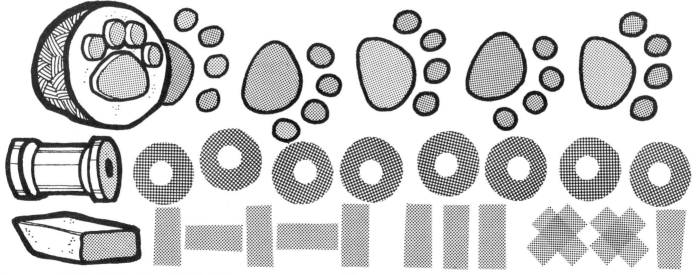

Name _____

Leaf Prints

What You Need

leaves with prominent veins
paper towels
newspapers
colored inks, tempera paints, *or* watercolors
plastic ice tray, muffin tin, *or* other small containers for paints
water
shallow, wide-mouthed container for water
liquid soap
paintbrushes
one 12″ x 18″ sheet of manila paper
felt-tipped marking pens
white glue
colored construction paper

What You Do

1. Wash your leaves and blot them dry with paper towels.
2. Cover your work surface with newspapers.
3. Pour paints or inks into containers.
4. If you are using tempera paints or watercolors, add a little liquid soap to the water so that the color will stick to the leaf.
5. Fold your manila paper in half and then open it.
6. Paint the veined side of a leaf with ink, tempera paint, or watercolor.
7. Place the leaf on one-half of the manila paper and fold the other half over it.
8. Using a book or other flat, heavy object, press the leaf between the sheets of manila paper for 5 to 10 seconds.
9. Open the folded paper and remove the leaf.
10. Repeat steps 6, 7, 8, and 9, each time placing the painted leaf on another part of your paper. Overlapping the leaves will give an added dimension to this project.
11. When your design is complete, allow the ink to dry for 10 to 15 minutes.
12. *(Optional)* With a fine-tipped marking pen, outline the printed leaves.
13. Glue your leaf print to a piece of construction paper. For best results, the construction paper should be of a complementary color and just enough larger than your print to form both a backing and a frame for it.

Variation

Use different papers for different effects. For example, you may want to try tissue paper, parchment, or rice paper for an Oriental effect.

Name _____

Sandpaper Prints

What You Need

one 7" x 10" piece of sandpaper of medium to fine texture
one 7" x 10" piece of construction paper
scissors
crayons
newspapers
iron
white glue
one 12" x 18" piece of construction paper of a different color
felt-tipped marking pens

What You Do

1. Using crayons, draw a picture or design on the rough side of the sandpaper. Color it in heavily.
2. Lay the construction paper on several thicknesses of newspaper.
3. Place the sandpaper face down on the construction paper.
4. Turn on the iron and set the temperature control on **medium**.
5. Hold the iron on the back of the sandpaper to transfer the crayon design to the construction paper beneath it.
6. Glue the sandpaper and the printed construction paper side by side on a large sheet of colored construction paper.
7. *(Optional)* Using felt-tipped marking pens, outline some parts of the design.

Draw on the rough side of the sandpaper with a crayon.

Use an iron to transfer the crayon drawing to a piece of construction paper.

Mount the sandpaper drawing and the construction paper print side by side on a piece of construction paper.

Name _____

Block Printing

What You Need

stiff paper or tagboard
pencil
scissors
rubber inner tube, thick cork, *or* thick cardboard
white glue
a square or rectangle of wood, plexi-glass, or tile
water soluble inks in a variety of colors
one piece of plate glass
brayer
printing paper (construction paper, newsprint, watercolor paper)
construction paper

What You Do

1. On stiff paper or tagboard, draw some shapes you wish to print. Simple shapes, such as a tree, an animal, a leaf, or a geometric shape, work best.
2. Cut out the shapes you have drawn.
3. Lay these shapes on the rubber, cork, or cardboard; draw around each; and cut them out.
4. Glue these cutout shapes firmly to the wood, plexi-glass, or tile to create a printing block.
5. Put ink on the glass plate and roll it with the brayer until it is evenly spread.
6. Using the brayer, apply ink evenly to your printing block.
7. Pick up the block, turn it over, and press the inked surface onto the printing paper.
8. Repeat steps 5, 6, and 7. Use different blocks or use the same block but different colors of ink. Wash excess ink from the glass, printing block, and brayer before applying another color.
9. When you have finished your block print, allow the ink to dry.
10. Glue your block print onto a larger piece of construction paper.
11. Display your framed print on a bulletin board or wall.

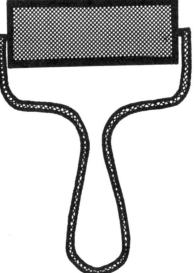